WITH BATED BREATH

WITH BATED BREATH

Bryden MacDonald

Talonbooks

Talonbooks
P.O. Box 2076, Vancouver, British Columbia, Canada V6B 3S3
www.talonbooks.com

Typeset in Scala and printed and bound in Canada.
Printed on 100% post-consumer recycled paper.

First Printing: 2010

The publisher gratefully acknowledges the financial support of the Canada
Council for the Arts; the Government of Canada through the Book
Publishing Industry Development Program; and the Province of British
Columbia through the British Columbia Arts Council and the Book
Publishing Tax Credit for our publishing activities.

LIBRARY AND ARCHIVES CANADA CATALOGUING IN PUBLICATION

MacDonald, Bryden, 1960–
    With bated breath / Bryden MacDonald.

A play.
ISBN 978-0-88922-651-7

    I. Title.

PS8575.D62W58 2010   C812'.54   C2010-902242-4

Here you come again
Just when I've begun to get myself together
You waltz right in the door
Just like you've done before
And wrap my heart
Round your little finger.

– Dolly Parton

With Bated Breath was first produced by Centaur Theatre Company in Montreal on April 21, 2009 with the following cast and crew:

ESTA:	Sarah Carlsen
WILLY:	Michael Sutherland-Young
FLOAT:	Éloi Archambaudoin
BERNIE:	Neil Napier
RICOTTA:	Danette Mackay
CAMILLA:	Felicia Shulman

Directed by Bryden MacDonald & Roy Surette

Set and Costume Design by James Lavoie
Lighting Design by Spike Lyne
Sound Design by Peter Cerone
Stage Manager: Todd Bricker

I would like to thank The Canada Council for the Arts, The Conseil des arts et des lettres; Jenny Munday and The Playwrights Atlantic Resource Centre, Emma Tibaldo and Greg MacArthur at Playwrights' Workshop Montreal, Paula Danckert at The National Arts Centre, and Jennifer Brewin and everyone at the Magnetic North Festival in beautiful St. John's. Thanks also to Stephen Willems at MCC theatre NY, Tony Taccone at The Berkeley Repertory Theatre, Maureen LaBonte, Robert Joy, Daniel MacIvor, Hugo Dann, Douglas Campbell, Lorne Pardy, Catherine Knights, and all the wonderful artists who took some part in the development of this play over the years.

A special thank you to Roy Surette for programming this play, supplying me with such a wonderful cast and design team, giving me the creative freedom to explore the play, and helping me with his invaluable insight, to bring it to the stage.

And thank you to a truly beautiful group of actors – brave souls indeed: Sarah, Michael, Éloi, Neil, Danette and Felicia.

AUTHOR'S NOTE

My plays are about journeys and rebirth – their endings bring new beginnings. They often shed light on those society has forgotten; those, who for one reason or another have found themselves trapped – and what happens when these people are set free.

In *With Bated Breath*, memory plays a prominent role: how time affects it, how it fractures and is often reinvented depending on the situation – and why is it that certain things stay with us with a blistering clarity, while other things simply slip away only to reveal themselves again later without warning.

One of my many guilty pleasures is country music, when it was really country music: the heightened heartache of Tammy Wynette and George Jones; Johnny Cash, Waylon Jennings, Tanya Tucker, and my all time fave Dolly Parton. *With Bated Breath* could easily be subtitled "a hurtin song." The broken characters in this play, with their double lives and tarnished armor, who sometimes only have their sense of humour to keep them afloat, are my heroes.

Cast in Order of Appearance

Esta: 27.

Willy: 19.

Float: 26.

Bernie: 45.

Ricotta: 43.

Camilla: 43.

An open space.
Shapes and shadows.

A stage on a stage.

A beaded curtain
crystalline
dominates the playing area.

Certainly
wherever we are
at any given time
we are only ever really almost there.

It's a blustery day
early autumn
on Cape Breton Island.

"I Will Always Love You"
by Dolly Parton
plays
as the clouds
in an accelerated fashion
alternately cover
and reveal the sun.

There is a clear break in the sky.
ESTA SNOW is revealed.

Eyes closed
she is on the edge of a cliff
that looks out over the ocean.
She clutches a bunch
of wild irises.

ESTA is in her mid-twenties:
a sweet
weary young woman –
pretty
plump.
Dressed simply
in bright colours.

Pause on this.
The music fades.
ESTA breathes in the fresh salty air.

ESTA:

    Dear Willy –
here I am writing to you in my head.
Praying sort of. I mean
the only other option is not to.
All the other stuff in between is too complex.
So I choose to pray.

Robby's good.
He's good with the kids.
He's a great dad – when he can play.
I'm still the bad cop.
But he's not drinkin as much but –
every now and again
just when things are goin okay
he skips the groceries and comes home pissed.
Happy as a lark.
He's never violent.
I should be glad for that.
But at the same time
I got three kids in one bed
told to pray their hunger away.
And I'm so mad at him.
I'm so mad at him I can't speak.

Truth be told –
me and Robby aren't doin much for each other.
But you know that.
And we know that.
We love each other and we get through it but.
Well.
No one's to blame really.
I'm sure I'm no treat to live with.
And for all his faults
and there really aren't many
he's better with the boys than I am.

I just don't seem to have the patience.
Seems I spend the bulk of my time
just watchin them spin out of control.
They're awful cute though.
I just don't know where they came from half the time.

I'd be better for them
when they're older I think.
The teenage years I think I could handle better.
They could handle me better.
I'd be better as their friend.
I'm not much of a mother.

> *She sniffs the flowers*
> *brushing her cheek with the bouquet.*

Camilla is worse and worse.
I'm afraid she's completely fucked.
Head over heels in love with herself.
Not a kind word to say about anyone.
And her problems –
they're all somebody else's fault:
she's a blame seeker in the first degree.
I visit her less and less.
And I feel bad about that –
I mean I'm just about the last friend she got left but
I can't take the deceitfulness –
how blasé she is about everything.
Even watchin the news with her –
especially since all the big disasters:
she's always disappointed in the body count.
Negative negative all the time.
I know I'm over-sensitive but.
It's all a bit much.

I can't say I don't think about leavin –
just pickin up and runnin away from it all.

I'd be lyin if I did.
You were brave to just leave.
To move on. I mean –
if I could just go away for a while
figure myself out a bit –
get better.
Get better and then come back with –
some little gifts of wisdom maybe
about survival and –
and life and –
something. Anything.
The boys would be happy to see me.
And Robby would be happy with someone else.
And I could be alone:
I would never get tired of that.

Just look at me suffer eh.
Oh yeah –
I'm a good sufferer.

Your wild irises are everywhere this year Willy.
And in September – it's the strangest thing.
Friggin global warming.
Or a miracle:
a sign from you is what I like to think.

I don't understand the people
who want to destroy this amazing world.
Can't wrap my head around that at all.
I feel like I should do more –
fight back in some way
somehow.
But it's tough to fight somethin you don't understand.
But I guess that's their plan:
keep us confused
keep us scared.
Stupid people.

Stupid people makin stupid decisions
right across the board.
Anyway.
Blah blah blah.

She acknowledges the flowers.

Really Willy
they're magnificent:
as plentiful as clover –
a blanket of purple.
The simple things eh.
Profound really –
when beauty can break your heart.

Happy birthday Willy.

She closes her eyes.

Be safe be safe be safe.

*She tosses the flowers
into the air
into the ocean.*

*Beyond the beaded curtain
WILLY PORTER is revealed.
He is a slim
pretty
boyish young man
wearing baggy jeans
and a blue hooded sweatshirt.
He sits in his favourite chair
his back straight
hands crossed at the wrists
in his lap.*

WILLY stands.
He comes through the beaded curtain.
The strands shimmer
tinkle and click.
ESTA smiles.

WILLY:

A rogue wave
almost snatched me away here once.

ESTA
still smiling
eyes still closed
gasps with delight.
WILLY moves to join her.

It was definitely here.
It was definitely on the east coast.
It wasn't the Pacific Ocean.
It was definitely the Atlantic.
The Pacific is more forgiving –
predictable even.
The Atlantic is more of a threat:
it's sexy that way.

ESTA's eyes remain closed.

ESTA:

It's so nice to hear your voice.

WILLY:

That's all I really know about oceans:
and only from the shore.

ESTA:

I don't know what I'd do without the ocean.

WILLY:

> I was standing on a cliff.
> Like this one.
> Maybe this same one.
> One second I was dry.
> The next I was wet.
> It's like they say it is:
> a wall of water –
> there and gone in a flash.
>
> Drenched to the skin.
> Wide awake suddenly –
> like jolted from sleep.
> but I wasn't asleep.
> I was awake.
> But it was like I –
> I don't know
> I mean I know I was awake but
> it's like I woke up from being awake
> to being more awake.
> Crazy. Ya know?
> And since then I can't help but think –
> what is awake?
> Ya know?
> Are we ever really awake?

ESTA:

> I hope not –
> I'd have no hope at all otherwise.

WILLY:

> It's so beautiful here.
> The danger kinda turns me on. I mean –
> sometimes
> it takes all the energy I have
> not to just throw myself in.

ESTA:
I feel that way around bonfires!

WILLY:
And sometimes I feel
I could just be sucked into a crack in the pavement
or pulled into the sky at any minute.

ESTA:
If you only had one word to describe the sky –
what would it be?
don't think too much.

WILLY:
Open.

ESTA:
Definitely.
Open.
That's what I was thinking too.

WILLY:
Open.

Silence.

ESTA:
Will you ever come back Willy?

WILLY:
I'll come back
to be swept away
by that tall dark handsome Rogue wave.
What a name for a wave eh –
Rogue.

ESTA:
Rogue.

They giggle.
WILLY is gone.
ESTA opens her eyes.
A sad smile.
She hugs herself.

Waves crash.
Gulls screech.

Music in:
Dolly Parton's working class anthem
"Nine to Five."

ESTA is gone.

A strip joint in Montreal:
Stud Cité.

FLOAT
cuts through the beaded curtain.

He is a buff
smooth-skinned young stud
full of coked-up energy.
He wears a summer white
U.S. Naval Academy jacket
and a first rank captain's white hat.
other than that —
skimpy professional underwear
and runners.
His strip tease isn't much of a tease —
the cap and jacket
come off almost immediately
and are tossed across the stage.
He's got rhythm and he works it.
His movements are choreographed and muscular
with emphasis

on flashing and slapping his ass
staring into his underwear
and feeling around
like a kid with a grab bag of candy.

He is absolutely charming
confident
and in love with his body.

FLOAT finishes his routine
blows kisses
and is gone before the song is over.

The music fades
into something more ambient:
Slutty and repetitive.

BERNIE GILLIS appears
leaning at the bar
alone at Stud Cité
getting pissed
staring into his drink –
the brim of his ball cap
almost touching the rim of his glass.

He's a strapping guy.
Forties.
No gym rat
but strong from hard work.
Blue jeans
work boots
t-shirt.

He raises his head
and suddenly
he's thinking out loud.

BERNIE:
Rob a bank.
Go to Vegas.
Bet everything.
Drink everything.
Fuck everything.
Lose everything.
Go to the desert.
Eat sand.
Pass out.
Wake up paralyzed from the neck down
and think myself to death
while the buzzards circle.

>*He downs his drink.*

Options.

>*He whispers:*

Fuck.
Fuck. Help. Fuck.
Fuck.

>*FLOAT appears.*
>*He is Francophone.*
>*He speaks English fluently*
>*with a very slight seductive accent*
>*though the accent is thicker when roping in a client.*

FLOAT:
Salut beauté
à qui tu parles?

BERNIE:
What?
FLOAT:
Hello Handsome –
who are you talking to?

BERNIE:
　Myself I guess.

FLOAT:
　Did you see my show?

BERNIE:
　Yes.
　You're very talented.

FLOAT:
　Thank you.
　I never see you here before.

BERNIE:
　Never been.

FLOAT:
　Where are you from?

BERNIE:
　Cape Breton Island.

FLOAT:
　Ooooo –
　The States.

BERNIE:
　Cape Breton Island.
　You never heard of Cape Breton Island?

FLOAT:
　No.

BERNIE:
　You must be a Member of Parliament.

　　He cracks himself up.

Casual dress on The Hill these days.

FLOAT:
> Je viens de Matane.
> Sais-tu où c'est ça?
> Non?
> C'est ce que je pensais.

BERNIE:
> I don't speak –

FLOAT:
> I'm from Matane.
> Do you have any idea where that is? No?
> I didn't think so.

BERNIE:
> I'm sorry.
> I'm an asshole.
> I've always wanted to learn French.

FLOAT:
> That's what you all say.
> But you never do.
> Pas de problème.
> We're here to have fun.
> You're a handsome guy.
> How old are you?

BERNIE:
> Thirty-four.
> Thirty-nine.
> Forty-five next month.
> You?

FLOAT:
> I have twenty-six years.
> You don't look forty-five.

BERNIE:
> You look twenty-six.

FLOAT pats BERNIE's stomach.

FLOAT:
> You're in awesome shape.
> I give you thirty –
> not more.

BERNIE:
> I'm really about fifteen.
> When I turned forty
> I started counting backwards in fives.
> I'm haggard jailbait.

FLOAT:
> You must work out.

BERNIE:
> Well – I work.
> And I work outside.
> So I guess I work out.

FLOAT:
> What do you do?

BERNIE:
> I'm a farmer.

FLOAT:
> That's sexy.

BERNIE:
> If you think miles of chicken shit is sexy.

FLOAT laughs.

FLOAT:
> I like you.

BERNIE:
> It's your job to like me.

FLOAT:
> I'll take you for a dance.
> You'll feel better.
> You want to relax with me?

BERNIE:
> Are you gay?

FLOAT:
> I'm gay until closing time.

BERNIE:
> I'm not gay either.
> I'm just fucked up.
> Really deeply fucked up.

FLOAT:
> You're a sexy guy.
> We get a lot of old queens in here –
> bitchy fags and Daddies.
> You're different.
> There's something different about you –
> something special I think.

BERNIE:
> And I think
> you're the worst pathological liar I've ever met.

FLOAT cuddles in close to BERNIE.

FLOAT:
> Come back to my office –
> you can tell me everything.

BERNIE:
> I need more booze.

FLOAT:
> Can you offer me a drink?
> I'm more fun when I have a little drink.

Then I'll take you for a dance.
You won't be disappointed.

BERNIE:
Well.
When in Rome.

> BERNIE *digs for money*
> *looking about the room.*

Where's the guy?

> FLOAT *plucks a twenty from* BERNIE's *hand.*

FLOAT:
I'll get it.
Same thing?

BERNIE:
Again and again.

FLOAT:
I'll be right back.
Stay where you are.
And smile.
You have a nice smile.

> FLOAT *is gone.*
> *Silence.*

BERNIE:
I'm a fuckin liar –
a loser and a fool.

Hate is easy.
Love is hard.
Love is inside a book.
Love is something you read about.
Love is fiction.

When did it happen?
How did it happen?
Why didn't I see it?
Now what?
Where should I go?
To the streets?
Will I find you in the streets?
If I did
would it matter?
I'm sorry means nothing.
I've been saying I'm sorry all my life.
I've never meant it.

I'm always in the same place:
I can leave the room
I can leave the country –
but I'm always in the same place.
It's always the same.
Like buddy with the big rock:
pushes it up the mountain
it rolls back down
pushes it up the mountain
it rolls back down.

Poor me.

> WILLY *is heard*
> *but not seen.*

WILLY:
I love you Mr. Gillis.

BERNIE:
I love you.

> FLOAT *appears with drinks.*

FLOAT:
>   But we just met.

BERNIE:
>   What?

FLOAT:
>   You can love me.
>   I was made to be loved.
>   I'm a love machine.

BERNIE:
>   You pretend you love me
>   and I'll pretend I'm rich.
>   Cheers.

FLOAT:
>   Santé.

>   *They toast.*
>   *Drink.*

BERNIE:
>   What's your name?

FLOAT:
>   Float.

BERNIE:
>   Float?

FLOAT:
>   Like in a boat.
>   I float.

BERNIE:
>   That's not your real name.

FLOAT:
>   It's the only name you need to know.
>   That's who I am right now.

BERNIE:
I'll call you Willy.

FLOAT:
That's my name.
See how easy it is?
Now come.
You want to be alone with me.
I know you do.
Don't be shy.
Life's too short.
Follow me.

FLOAT moves to the shadows.
BERNIE alone.

WILLY is heard
but not seen.

WILLY:
I love you Mr. Gillis.

BERNIE:
Willy?

BERNIE follows the sound of WILLY's voice.
He sits in a nearby chair.

Beyond the beaded curtain
WILLY is revealed.
In his chair
hands crossed at the wrists
in his lap.

WILLY stands.
He comes through the beaded curtain
and moves towards BERNIE.

Hi Willy.
How are you baby?

WILLY sits on BERNIE's knee.

WILLY & FLOAT:
I'm horny.

WILLY:
I miss you.

BERNIE:
I love you.

WILLY:
I love you.

BERNIE:
Do you remember the first time you said you loved me?

WILLY:
Yes.

BERNIE:
You said you loved me.
I looked into your eyes.
I saw myself.
I dismissed you.

WILLY:
That's okay.

BERNIE:
My heart froze up.
My heart froze up
like the pipes in a deserted farm house
in the dead of a cliché Canadian winter.

WILLY:
That would hurt.

BERNIE:
>Fuckin right it did.
>It still does.
>It hurts every day.

WILLY:
>We're together now.

BERNIE:
>What colour are your eyes?

WILLY & FLOAT:
>What colour do you want them?

>*BERNIE stares into WILLY's eyes for a few moments.*

BERNIE:
>There.
>That's perfect.
>They're beautiful.
>You're beautiful.

WILLY & FLOAT:
>Thank you.

BERNIE:
>Can you forgive me?

WILLY:
>For what Mr. Gillis?

BERNIE:
>For being wrong.
>For lying.

WILLY:
>Don't worry about that Mr. Gillis.

WILLY & FLOAT:
>We're all liars here.

BERNIE:
Dance for me?

WILLY & FLOAT:
It would be my pleasure.

Music in:
"Danger Ahead"
by Tanya Tucker.

WILLY begins to dance for BERNIE
unzipping his sweatshirt
and dropping it on the floor.
Then WILLY is replaced by FLOAT
who continues
with a more aggressive seduction.
WILLY is gone.

Then
abruptly
music out.
FLOAT is gone.

BERNIE alone.
He picks up WILLY's sweatshirt from the floor.
He stares at it a moment
buries his face in it
inhaling deeply
then holds it to his chest.

RICOTTA CHISHOLM appears.
She is a sexy hardbitten woman
in her mid-forties.
Dressed for work.
Comfortably conservative.
Barefoot.

RICOTTA:

Where's Willy?

BERNIE:

He said he had to go.
He forgot he had to go.

RICOTTA:

He can't walk that far.

BERNIE:

He said he wanted to.

RICOTTA:

What did you say to him?

BERNIE:

Nothing.
He had to go.
He said he had to go.
He forgot his sweatshirt.

RICOTTA:

It's mild out.

She takes the sweatshirt from BERNIE.

What did he say?
What did he say to you?

BERNIE:

He said he had to go.
And he went.

RICOTTA:

Something is goin on.
I don't know.
Well –
I hope you're hungry.

RICOTTA is gone.
BERNIE alone.

WILLY appears
in a shard of light.
BERNIE is gone.

WILLY:
　　I miss you.
　　And I miss the sound
　　of the coyotes after a kill –
　　their howls ricocheting across the lake.
　　And I miss the wild irises –
　　hanging onto the craggy rocks
　　on the cliffs of Lighthouse Point:
　　the waves crashing
　　and the winds blowing.
　　It's amazing how strong those little flowers are.
　　But there's lots of ways to be strong –
　　surrender is one.

　　　　BERNIE is heard
　　　　but not seen.

BERNIE:
　　Where are you?

WILLY:
　　I'm in the loft.
　　In the barn.

　　I went to the barn everyday.
　　Going to the barn was like going to church.
　　The barn was my church.

　　There's a window in the loft
　　shaped like a stop sign
　　tucked in a little A-frame alcove.

I stacked bales of hay
to climb up to the window to see through.

Looking through that window for the first time
was like looking through a telescope.
Everything that had been familiar –
the mountain the river the clouds –
seemed new from up there.
And I could see the roof of your house:
corrugated copper
like a gold green lagoon in the sky.

Up there
I told secrets to myself
swearing myself to secrecy.
I took my clothes off to confess.
The itchy hay became a comfort.
And everyday I prayed for a better world.
And everyday I planned my escape.
And everyday
after the prayers
I jerked off on a blue and white striped gardening glove
that I stole off the seat
of your riding lawn mower.

A spider became my only friend.
Eventually
when I won her trust
she spun her web over my face
and sat just under my eyebrow.
I could feel her shadow –
waiting.
She spun her first fly
just under my nose.
When I breathed it shimmered.

I was safe then.
I'm safe now.
I'll be fine.
I'm fine.

> *Music in:*
> *"Save the Last Dance for Me"*
> *by Dolly Parton.*

> *WILLY smiles.*
> *He watches*
> *as BERNIE arrives at a Toronto tavern.*
> *BERNIE sits at a table*
> *and opens a paperback novel.*
> *WILLY comes from the shadows*
> *not seen by BERNIE*
> *and places a glass of rye for him.*
> *BERNIE*
> *still reading*
> *reaches for the glass –*
> *their hands almost touch.*
> *WILLY is gone.*
> *BERNIE drinks and reads.*

> *Music out.*
> *RICOTTA is heard.*

RICOTTA:
Get a fucking life why doncha!
And get the fuck out of mine while you're at it!

> *RICOTTA appears.*
> *She carries a half-finished jug of draft*
> *and a beer glass.*
> *A London Fog-like trench coat.*
> *A large overstuffed purse slung over her shoulder.*
> *She wears dark glasses.*

She lands at the bar
a short distance from BERNIE.
BERNIE *glances.*

RICOTTA:
Pardon my bravado.
But honest ta fuck –
some of those girls are scarier than the guys
sometimes.

> BERNIE *smiles*
> *and continues to read.*
> RICOTTA *tries to suppress a burp*
> *but can't.*

Fuck.
Excuse me.
I'm mortified.
Really.

> *She digs a bottle of tomato juice from her purse*
> *opens it*
> *and mixes herself a Redeye.*

What are you reading?

BERNIE:
I um – I found it here –
it was just laying on the table.

> *He displays the cover.*

The Silence of the Lambs.

RICOTTA:
I love a good comedy.

She coughs
almost hacking up a lung.
She recovers.

Christ. Excuse me.
I know what you're thinking:
who's the sexy girl? right?
I'm a little under the weather today.
Anyway –

She joins him
removing her coat
and flinging her bag over the back of her chair.

I'm awake now.
Um –
one more question for you
then maybe I'll leave you alone:
where am I?
Toronto. I know I'm in Toronto.
But um ya know – big town.
So just um – generally where am I?

BERNIE:
East end.
Two maybe three blocks south of here
you can grab a streetcar west –
take you right over to Yonge and Queen.

RICOTTA:
Thank you.
And it's Saturday.

BERNIE:
All day.

RICOTTA:
What's your name?
You really don't wanna read that book.

BERNIE:
    Not really.
    Bernie.
    You?

RICOTTA:
    Ricotta.
    Don't ask.
    Call me Ric.
    Pleasure.

        She extends her hand.
        They shake.

BERNIE:
    Nice to meet you.

RICOTTA:
    You're very handsome.
    Are you gay?
    Sorry.
    You don't have to answer that.
    You're gay aren't you.
    Is this a gay bar?

BERNIE:
    I don't think so.
    I don't know.

        She looks about
        peeking gingerly over her glasses.

RICOTTA:
    This is a gay bar.
    A very unpopular one.
    But. Figures.
    Leave it to me.
    Fag hag. Sometimes dyke.

Actually I have no idea how I "identify":
the well of loneliness knows no gender –
a rose is a rose.
But the men I want are queer
and the women I want are straight
so ultimately it's just a big cosmic joke.
That's my latest justification for afternoon drinking.
You?

BERNIE:

I'm not really – anything.
I'm kind of just –
overexposed and underused.
I don't really fit.
But if you were holding a gun to my head
I'd have to say that I'm an alcoholic first.

RICOTTA:

A man with priorities.
Cheers.

They toast and drink.

My fag friends are sick of the gay scene.
They all hang out in straight bars.
Apparently it's the only way to get laid.
Then again
that's Russell who says that
and he'd fuck a wet stick.
I do question him when he says that.
Has that been your experience?

BERNIE:

I don't even know you.

RICOTTA:

Happens all the time.
I'm easy to talk to apparently.

People feel comfortable with me.
I don't know why
cuz I scare the shit out of myself.
But people just tell me things.
Years of being a bartender I guess.
I don't know. Sorry. Look –
you're gonna have to excuse me.
I can't seem to shut up. But –
I did coke last night.
I haven't done coke since –
I was like twelve.
It really is a young person's drug.
Christ – listen to me.
I'm not always like this. Well –
yes I am. Lately.
My life is falling apart.
My father finally died:
five by-passes and a wooden leg later.
God rest him
but he was a miserable prick.
I'm the goddamn executor of the goddamn will.
I inherited the farm.
If you can call it that:
a chicken farm that makes Hooterville
look like the McCain Estates.
It'll be like goin back
to a goddamn high school reunion.
Anyway. Excuse me.
Really.

BERNIE:

I'm gonna go out on a limb here:
are you from the east coast?

RICOTTA:
>   Cape Breton Island:
>   born and derailed.
>   But I'm not the best representation
>   of the good people of the Island:
>   I hate the fuckin fiddle.

BERNIE:
>   I lived in Halifax most of my life
>   but my family is from Cape Breton.

RICOTTA:
>   Fuck off.
>   Where?

BERNIE:
>   Upper Grand Mira area.
>   Gillises.

RICOTTA:
>   Vincent?

BERNIE:
>   I had an Uncle Vincent.

RICOTTA:
>   Married about four times?
>   A scandal the second time –
>   married his ex-wife's sister.

BERNIE:
>   Maybelle.

RICOTTA:
>   That's right.
>   Maybelle.
>   She was trouble for a little old lady.

BERNIE:
>   No flies on her.

RICOTTA:
He owned a hardware store on Grand Lake Road?

BERNIE:
That's him.

RICOTTA:
I worked there one summer as a cashier.
Well what d'ya know.

BERNIE:
What d'ya know.
Vincent.
We looked up to him eh.
Us young guys –
cuz he was such a hooligan.
Sly bastard. Charm for days.
Free spirit for sure.

RICOTTA:
Ah Vincent.
We're Chisholms though.
My mother was Wanda Keeping.
The Roaches Road Keepings.
New Waterford.

BERNIE:
Tough town.

RICOTTA:
Good people.

> *She takes off her glasses.*
> *She is momentarily blinded.*
> *She looks about the room.*

Well –
this place is dead.

BERNIE:
It's only noon.

RICOTTA:
Don't remind me.
Can I get you a drink?

BERNIE:
Sure.

RICOTTA:
What's your poison?

BERNIE:
Rye. Ice.

She digs in her purse
pulls out two mini bottles
and checks the labels.

RICOTTA:
I got Smirnoff and Wild Turkey.
Turkey for you.
Smir for me.
But no ice.
I'm not refrigerated yet.
There's the retirement plan:
invent a refrigerated purse –
but it can't be too heavy.

BERNIE:
And it's gotta look great.

RICOTTA:
Damn right.

They laugh
rebooting their drinks
avoiding suspicious eyes.

What do you do?

BERNIE:
Jack of all trades.
I'm pretty much reinvented
by the moment
on the spot.
Doin a bit of contract construction right now

RICOTTA:
Well I'm lookin for a handy man.

She leans in and kisses him.
They neck.

Where can we get a good greasy breakfast around here?

BERNIE:
Not far.

RICOTTA:
Any fear of me
ever havin to stare into your devilish eyes again
after I'm through with you today?

BERNIE:
I'm pretty easy.

RICOTTA:
You got money for a cab?

BERNIE:
Yep.

RICOTTA:
You got all the right answers.

Music in:
"Whose Bed Have Your Boots Been Under"
by Shania Twain.
RICOTTA and BERNIE neck.
A stylized
acrobatic
make-out session ensues
with laughing all the way.
BERNIE mounts RICOTTA
spreadeagled on the table —
she claws his back
bites his ear
and pulls off his shirt.
An impressive flip
finds RICOTTA on top.
BERNIE cups her breasts
then removes her dress
quickly and with ease.
BERNIE practically leaps from the table
with RICOTTA straddling his waist.
Joined as one
they gather clothes
almost forgetting RICOTTA's bag.
Then
as the music fades into
Dolly Parton's
"Single Bars and Single Women"
BERNIE carries RICOTTA
through the beaded curtain
in a warm embrace.
Then
BERNIE is gone.

RICOTTA alone
beyond the beaded curtain

in black bra
panties and heels
recalls a time of burlesque.
She moves with the music
slowly and seductively
using the beaded curtain as her partner:
a beautiful
woebegone display.
Then
from the shadows
WILLY holds up a simple cotton dress.
RICOTTA slips into this effortlessly
as if it is being poured over her.

WILLY is gone.
RICOTTA removes her shoes
and collects a glass of scotch.

The music fades
into the yelps of coyotes
then the barking of a lone dog
and the plaintive cry of loons.

RICOTTA comes through the beaded curtain
appearing on her dilapidated veranda.

It is nearing dusk.
She sips scotch.
She is lost in pleasant memory.
She smiles.
A little laugh.
Then
She is sky-gazing.
She smells something in a breeze.

RICOTTA:
    The first sweet sharp smell of autumn –
    and right on time.

        A sigh.

    Autumn is the time of year to fall in love.
    Not summertime.
    Summertime is too demanding.
    Too arrogant.
    It squashes the shy ones.
    The shy ones have a chance in autumn.
    Springtime is too fickle
    and winter is time to reflect.
    Autumn is the time of year to fall in love.

        She sips her scotch.
        She muses.
        She smiles
        watching the clouds mutate above her.

    Two barely white clouds
    on a barely grey sky.

    Two long canoes.
    No.
    They're melding.
    It's a gondola.
    Like I've ever seen a fucking gondola before –
    but there one is.
    And –
    full of guests suddenly ta boot:
    gals with parasols guys in capes –
    a sword fight in a dress shop. No –
    it's a tango. Fuck –
    it's the civil war:
    the south is burning –

all those prissy bitches
trying to run in those big stupid hoop skirts.
No. No wait.
Oh that's better – yum yum
men in kilts:
the battle of Culloden.

She giggles and sips her scotch.

Gondola gone.
Nooooow. Now now now it's –
it's a –
tropical island: a botanical garden in a wisp of smoke.
Manet Monet –
who was the flower guy?
Were they both going blind?
Who painted those beautiful blurry flowers?

Gentle rain is heard.

Ah rain.
It's too perfect:
light rain falling through flannel flowers.
Fuck. Fucking beautiful.
I could listen to the rain forever.
If I believed in heaven
it would always be raining.

A sip of scotch.
She muses.

I love the way the weather changes back here.
One of the main things
that drove us back from the city eh? Well –
drove me back anyway.
That
along with poverty and one too many blackout drunks.

She laughs.
A sip of scotch.
She muses.

Thunder tonight.
Hopefully lightning.

She is lost in the sky.
Then –

We should think about supper.

She looks about.

Bernie?
Where are you?
We should start thinking about supper.
Bernie?

Bernie where are you?

Silence.

She remembers.
She becomes short of breath.
She screams BERNIE's name.
A clap of thunder.
A bolt of lightning.
A dog barks a warning.
The coyotes howl.
RICOTTA is gone.

CAMILLA MILLEY
and ESTA appear
sitting at CAMILLA's kitchen table
sharing a pot of tea
listening to RICOTTA's distant screaming.

CAMILLA is forty-something,
strong and wiry.
She wears sweatpants and a t-shirt.
She doesn't wear a bra.
She doesn't own one.

ESTA:
Listen to her scream.

CAMILLA:
Fuckin banshee.

ESTA:
I hear her right across town sometimes.

CAMILLA:
Try livin across the road.

The screaming subsides.
A final howl from the dog.

ESTA:
I never bothered to ask before –
but what kind of name is Ricotta anyway?

CAMILLA:
She was named after her father's favourite cheese.

ESTA:
That's a sin.

CAMILLA:
Could be worse.

ESTA & CAMILLA:
Velveeta.

They high five.

ESTA:

It's like right out of a Stephen King book eh?
I don't mean to be uncharitable but –
she creeps me out.
She kinda scares me.

CAMILLA:

She's harmless.
Just nuts.
And loud.
But she was always a little touched.

ESTA:

God love her though.

CAMILLA:

God love us.
We gotta put up with it.
Does no good to call the cops.
She's sweet as pie when they arrive.

ESTA:

Is it true she blows thum?

CAMILLA:

I wouldn't put it past her.
But she's a dyke.

ESTA:

Ya think?

CAMILLA:

I know.
She tried to get me once.
Up the Saint Anthony Daniel dance.
High school.
We were drunk.
She wanted ta fool around.
Practically had ta beat her off.

But she wasn't crazy then.
Just loose. And dykey.

ESTA:

You never told me that.

CAMILLA:

No reason to.
Actually –
just remembered it.
Anyways
she doesn't even acknowledge me now.
Frosts me right out.

ESTA:

Maybe she's still embarrassed.

CAMILLA:

Well if that's the case
she should get over it.
We were kids. Nah –
it's more than that.
She doesn't acknowledge anyone.
And I can't be bothered.
I can play that game too.
She can't be trusted anyways.
She's always stealin from the Co-op.

ESTA:

She's had her problems.

CAMILLA:

No kiddin.
Her husband bein a fruit for starters.

ESTA:

Well everyone suspected that.
She musta known.
And if she's a dyke –

CAMILLA:
    She never admitted to anyone.
    So it would still be a shock
    if your husband turned queer
    even if you were pretendin not to be a dyke.

ESTA:
    True.
    I guess.
    But maybe they're bisexuals.
    That's so mysterious.
    They were together
    but not together together –
    like they had independent lives
    outside of who they were as a they.
    An arrangement.
    They're probably both bisexuals.

CAMILLA:
    Esta Snow –
    there's no such thing as bisexuals.

ESTA:
    Horseshit Camilla –
    They're all bisexuals up Montreal.

CAMILLA:
    No –
    they're all flirts up Montreal.
    There's a difference.
    There's straights
    and dykes
    and fags
    and flirts up Montreal.
    There's no such thing as bisexuals.

ESTA:
>	Oh please Camilla –
>	I think about women.
>	Don't tell me you don't.

CAMILLA:
>	That's different –
>	you're just thinking.

ESTA:
>	But I really think.

CAMILLA:
>	You're just a flirt Esta –
>	just like me.
>	We don't wanna have sex with women
>	and we hate sex with men.
>	We're flirts.
>	We're not bisexuals.
>	There's no such thing as bisexuals.

ESTA:
>	Oh for Christsake Camilla –

>	> *RICOTTA screams.*
>	> *The dog barks.*

>	Jesus! Fuck!

CAMILLA:
>	I know.
>	There oughta be a law.
>	And she hasn't been further than that veranda
>	in months eh.
>	Apparently she gets paralyzed with fear
>	if she tries to go beyond it.
>	Sends her straight to bed.
>	She's got all the doctors
>	wrapped around her little finger.

And no one can get near her
cuz of that demon dog of hers.
On guard day and night.
That dog never liked anyone but Ricotta.
Eerie how loyal that dog is.
And vicious.
She ate her young eh.
First and only litter.
Ate them all in one sitting.
Straight from hell that dog.
They deserve each other.
Her pissed out of her fuckin gourd
babblin away on that veranda
screamin for Bernie
cursin anyone who questions her
and that fuckin dog singin back-up.

ESTA:

That's sad though.
We're all so fragile eh.
Ya never know when it could all just snap.
My fear is it'll be in public:
a meltdown in the middle of the mall
or at parent-teacher night.

CAMILLA:

She was always a big drinker.
Even before Bernie took off.
I remember years ago
at Donalda Mercer's wedding reception –
Ricotta took a big swig of the candle –
thought it was her vodka and coke.
Burnt her whole upper lip
and scalded her neck from the wax.
No one said nothin –
she went screamin to the bathroom.

Never came back.
Climbed out the window I guess.

ESTA:
Probably.
Sad.
So lonely eh.

CAMILLA:
That's puttin it mildly.
But her grief is real I suppose –
even if she is a neurotic bitch.
Fuck. I don't know.
She loves the attention.
But the grief gets a hold of us all in different ways.
Like when Pappa died
Mumma just stopped cookin.
We kids would have starved
if it wasn't for the apple trees and the berries.
Imagine if he died in winter –
us way out there on Blacketts Lake Road:
dead –
we woulda been dead I tell ya.
Can't eat an apple to this day.
Another toke?

ESTA:
One more little one
then I gotta go get supper on.

   CAMILLA *lights a joint.*

Hard thing though
havin your guy run out on ya –
queer or not.
But there's more to all of that than we know.

CAMILLA:

    Damn right there is.
    Ya gotta admit
    it is pretty suspect
    Bernie disappearin
    just days after that little Porter tramp
    vanished into thin air up Montreal.

ESTA:

    Willy.
    His name is Willy.

CAMILLA:

    And what were they thinkin –
    invitin a kid like that into their home?

ESTA:

    They were being kind Camilla.
    And I don't wanna hear anything unsavoury
    about Willy –
    not in my presence.

CAMILLA:

    Well Esta dear –
    good sources say
    he got himself all mixed up with the Mafia.
    And they got the real Mafia up Montreal – oh yeah.
    Not like down home here
    when the odd barn cat
    gets nailed to a telephone pole.
    They got the real thing up Montreal.
    I heard some pervert used that rape drug on him.
    Some pervert
    dropped that rape drug in his drink or something.
    All they found was –

ESTA:
Camilla –
you're exaggerating.

CAMILLA:
Well –
people talk.

ESTA:
Don't they just.

CAMILLA:
And what is that supposed to mean?

ESTA:
People talk.
I agree.
And that's all it is –
talk.

CAMILLA:
You think I'm gossiping.
I do not make these things up.
I hear them.
Besides
I'm not above gossip.
There's truth in everything.

ESTA:
Yes there is.
And the truth is
Willy Porter is as sweet as can be.
Made you feel comfortable and important
like you were the only one in the room.

CAMILLA:
You gotta stop fallin in love with gays.

ESTA:
    I wasn't in love.
    We had a connection.

CAMILLA:
    Whatever.

ESTA:
    Whatever.
    He had a beautiful imagination.

CAMILLA:
    See?
    You think he's dead too.

ESTA:
    Has.
    Has a beautiful imagination.

CAMILLA:
    He was also suckin off drunks behind the Legion
    by the time he was fourteen years old.

ESTA:
    So what?
    You're no Snow-fuckin-White.
    You can be so hard Camilla.
    And what do you know.
    What do you really know anyway?

CAMILLA:
    I know most queers hate women.
    And they're only attracted to redneck arseholes –
    straight weirdos we wouldn't look twice at.
    They are rarely attracted to each other.

ESTA:
    It's moments like this Camilla
    when I wonder why the hell

I hang out with you.
Listen to yourself.

CAMILLA:
I call thum like I see thum.

ESTA:
You're blind.
Willy is different.
And he wasn't afraid to be different.
You just never bothered to look.
I remember the first night I met him
watchin him dance with Ursula Simms.
Beautiful dancer.

CAMILLA:
Yeah –
but it was probably ballroom or somethin.

ESTA:
Well it was pretty intricate –
but what the hell is that supposed ta mean?
He was bein nice –
dancin with Ursula when no one else would.
He understands the little things a woman appreciates.
It isn't always about sex ya know.

CAMILLA:
Ursula Simms.
Was she holdin a gun to his head?
She'd screw the nuts off an iron bridge.

ESTA:
For your information Camilla
Ursula's settled right down –
she's mended her ways.
Her and Stanley Gosbee are engaged.

CAMILLA:
    Stanley Gosbee?
    And Ursula Simms?
    Well –
    there's a murder-suicide waitin to happen.

ESTA:
    You are goin straight ta hell Camilla Milley.

CAMILLA:
    Who would I know in heaven?

ESTA:
    You're impossible.
    You're a harsh
    and hard woman.

CAMILLA:
    I'm hard cuz life is hard.
    I'm not under no illusions about that.
    But if I think my best friend
    is livin her life vicariously through a dead fruit
    then I'm gonna say it.
    I gotta be honest.
    People can't handle that –
    it's not my fuckin problem.
    I'm honest.

ESTA:
    You're a cold bitch is what you are.
    Who hurt you so bad?

CAMILLA:
    What the hell is that supposed ta mean?

ESTA:
    Dig deep Camilla.
    Dig deep into your own life for once
    instead of everyone else's.

CAMILLA:
Well excuse me but –

ESTA:
No.
You listen to me Camilla.
You listen very carefully.
You're not an easy friend.
But I stand by you.
I've stood by you when no one else would.
So you respect me.
You respect my opinions.
You respect my beliefs.
If you are going to continue to be my friend
you must respect me.
They do not know Willy is dead for sure.
No matter where all the fuckin arrows are pointin –
they do not know for sure
that Willy is dead.
Willy is my friend.
Stop talking about my friend like he's dead.

Silence.

CAMILLA:
I'm sorry.

ESTA:
I know.

Silence.

Willy has a voice all his own.
And for someone with no real voice
like me
that's very attractive.
All I ever had were
are

these busy crippling concrete thoughts.
But I know who I am and I know where I stand.
And knowing that
it's easier
and very enjoyable
to appreciate others' gifts.
I mean the weight of the world is enormous right?
I mean –
I'm not lazy.
We're not lazy.
It's just hard.
And we work hard.
And we try not to complain.
At least I do.

CAMILLA:

Bitch.

ESTA:

So we laugh.
Right?

CAMILLA:

Yes we do.

ESTA:

Laugh or die.

CAMILLA:

That's right.

> *Smiles.*
> *Silence.*

ESTA:

We have the same birthday eh –
me and Willy.
Did you know that?

CAMILLA:
> No.
> Maybe.

ESTA:
> That bonded us right away I gotta say.
> No that's not true.
> We bonded over a gram of hash
> at a lobster boil in Louisbourg.
> Neither of us ever met anyone with our birthday.
> And ya know what? Twice
> we got each other the very same birthday card.
> Once by mail
> when he went to that Jazz Dance Camp up Moncton.
> Whenever that was.
> Time. Fuck.

> *Silence.*

CAMILLA:
> Know what my little niece Diana said the other day?
> We were playin one of her games –
> Care Bear Candyland
> or some fuckin thing.
> And she's just starin at me
> with those big Audrey Hepburn eyes of hers.
> Then she points to my crow's feet –
> almost pokes my fuckin eye out –
> and says Auntie Milla
> what are they?
> I say they're my laugh lines.
> And without missin a beat she says:
> do they go away when you're sad?

ESTA:
> Ahhhh.

CAMILLA:
　　I know.
　　You wanna Rice Krispies square?

ESTA:
　　Yeah okay.
　　No. No no.
　　I had a pear earlier.

CAMILLA:
　　A pear?

ESTA:
　　Yes a pear.
　　And it was delicious.
　　I thought I let it sit on the counter too long but I didn't.
　　It was so sweet.
　　I sliced it thinly on no-salt saltines
　　with a bit of low-fat mozza.
　　It was beautiful.
　　So I'm fine.

CAMILLA:
　　Fine?
　　I'm worried about you dear.
　　Goin on a diet
　　givin up smoking and drinkin
　　all at the same time.
　　I think that's dangerous.

ESTA:
　　I'm still smoking joints.

CAMILLA:
　　I know.
　　Buy your own.

ESTA:
　　Fuck off.

CAMILLA:
　　I'm kiddin.

ESTA:
　　I know.

CAMILLA:
　　They say quittin smoking
　　is tougher than kickin heroin.

ESTA:
　　You mean I coulda been doin heroin all this time.

CAMILLA:
　　Crack too especially.
　　And Xanax.

ESTA:
　　I'm not givin up my Xanax.
　　I'm only on the baby pink ones.
　　They're colour-coded for strength.
　　It's like a strong Advil for crissake.

CAMILLA:
　　Oh I know all about it dear.
　　My Aunt Rita in Inverness started on pink.
　　She's on the black ones now.
　　She sits in front of the shopping channel day and night
　　in a catatonic stupor.
　　What's that all about?

ESTA:
　　Maybe one day
　　ya just get too scared.
　　And it's all out there –
　　things ta scare ya.
　　No shortage of that.

CAMILLA:
    No shortage of that.

ESTA:
    But I'm just on the pink ones
    and that's where I'm stayin.

    A stoned silence.

    I don't hate sex with men.

CAMILLA:
    Don't be crazy –
    yes ya do.
    Men around here?

ESTA:
    Oh I don't know. I mean –
    don't laugh but –
    I've been havin a recurring dream
    where Courtney Cox is eatin me out.

CAMILLA:
    Courtney Cox?

ESTA:
    I love her hair.

CAMILLA:
    Well she's got nice hair
    but that blonde one is more interesting.

ESTA:
    I don't like blondes.
    That's not true –
    Sharon Stone could do me.

CAMILLA:
    She's a stuck-up demented bitch.

ESTA:

She is not.
She's with Mensa and everything.
She got an IQ the size of Kelly's Mountain.
She's smart.
I can only have dyke fantasies if they're smart.

CAMILLA:

Well Courtney Cox is not smart.

ESTA:

She acted stupid on the show.
She's smart in real life.

CAMILLA:

Real life?
What do any of them know about real life?

ESTA:

True.
Fuck –
I gotta go.
The kids have turned into dingoes by now.
I'll call ya later –
if they haven't cut off the phone.

CAMILLA:

Take this roach with ya.

ESTA:

Thanks.

They hug.

CAMILLA:

Your hair smells nice today –
what's that?

ESTA:
  I put lemons in it.
  Tryin ta bring the natural highlights out in the sun.
  Read it somewheres. Saw it somewheres.
  I don't know.

CAMILLA:
  Smells nice.

ESTA:
  Thanks.

> CAMILLA *runs her fingers through* ESTA's *hair*
> *playing with it a bit.*

CAMILLA:
  It's got a nice length now too.

ESTA:
  If I can just hang in and not cut it.

CAMILLA:
  Be brave.

ESTA:
  Yeah.
  Okay. Later.

CAMILLA:
  Later.

> ESTA *is gone.*

> CAMILLA *alone.*
> *She sniffs her fingers*
> *then licks them.*

> *Music in:*
> *"Heartbreaker"*
> *by Dolly Parton.*

CAMILLA *clears the table*
and tucks the chairs into place.
RICOTTA *appears beyond the beaded curtain*
tarted up for the Saint Anthony Daniel dance
drinking from a pint bottle
swaying with the music.

CAMILLA *sees* RICOTTA.
CAMILLA *goes through the beaded curtain*
approaches RICOTTA *from behind*
and puts her hands over RICOTTA*'s eyes.*
RICOTTA *laughs*
and pulls CAMILLA*'s hands from her eyes.*
She turns to CAMILLA
and is happily surprised to see her.
They hug.
They share a drink.
A sexy silly
schoolgirl waltz ensues.
Then suddenly
CAMILLA *presses a passionate kiss on* RICOTTA*'s*
mouth.
Startled
RICOTTA *pulls away.*
She rejects CAMILLA *gently.*

RICOTTA *is gone.*
CAMILLA *alone.*

After a moment
CAMILLA *slices through the beaded curtain.*
She rolls down the waistband of her sweats
revealing the straps of a g-string
riding high on her hip bones.
With the empty face
of a jaded stripper —

squeezing her breasts
and rubbing her crotch —
she gyrates slowly to Dolly's lament.
She pulls her t-shirt off
twisting it in her hands
over her head
as if wringing out her heart.

She drops the shirt on the ground.
The music fades.
Then
CAMILLA is taking the sun
standing
eyes closed
face to the sky.

WILLY appears.
He sees CAMILLA.
Embarrassed
he averts his eyes.
He clears his throat.

Nonchalant
CAMILLA looks at him
staring him down for a moment.

CAMILLA:
  Oops.

  She covers her breasts
  casually with her hands.

I was just gettin a bit of sun.
I didn't think anyone was around.
Thought everyone went to town.
This is embarrassing.
I'm sorry.

WILLY:

Sorry. I um.

Hi.

I was just wondering –

do you need anything done around the yard?

I work for cheap.

CAMILLA:

That's what we hear dear.

WILLY:

Um –

I'm Willy.

CAMILLA:

I know who you are.

WILLY:

I know who you are too.

Hello Miss Milley.

CAMILLA:

Please. Camilla. So –

we're neighbours it seems.

WILLY:

For a while.

Till I get on my feet.

Bernie and Ric –

they've been great.

CAMILLA:

But you know what people are sayin of course.

WILLY:

No.

What?

CAMILLA:

    Just be careful.

    People aren't always what they seem.

    And with your background

    you really don't need anymore trouble do you?

WILLY:

    I don't know what you mean.

CAMILLA:

    Seems you and Bernie spend a lot of time alone.

WILLY:

    I help him around the farm.

    There's a lot to be done.

CAMILLA:

    Willy dear –

    I'm telling you this for your own good.

    Only because no one else is brave enough to.

    Their pasts are questionable.

    And she's the worst of the two.

    He gains your trust.

    Then she moves in.

    She likes –

    boys like you.

    I've seen it over and over again.

    People turn a blind eye.

    But she's dangerous.

    Pathological almost.

    It's sad really.

    And Bernie? Well –

    he couldn't give a shit about you.

    He just does what she says. He's –

    oh what's that crude term?

    Pussy whipped.

    And before you know it –

if you're not careful
you'll be in too deep.
I just don't want you to get hurt Willy.
No one does.
It's obvious you're trying to get your life back together.
It's been hard for you.
We know. We all know that.
Everyone wants the best for you –
after what you've been through.
Small towns may have bad reputations
but we do look out for each other.
So just consider this a heads up.
You'll figure it out I'm sure.
You seem like a bright young man.
Hopefully you'll know when to get out.
I suggest you get out soon.

She plants her hands firmly on her hips.

And just to be clear dear –
we never had this conversation.

Silence.

WILLY:
You know Miss Milley –
it takes even less energy
to be nice than it does to be mean.

And WILLY is gone.
CAMILLA alone.
Self-satisfied.
A brief moment of remorse.
She shrugs this off.
She picks up her shirt
and puts it on.

CAMILLA is gone.

ESTA appears
giggling
wearing a cute colourful bathrobe
and a dime store birthday hat.
She sits at the table
her eyes covered with her hands.

ESTA:
Okay!

> *She continues to giggle.*
> *WILLY appears*
> *wearing large sunglasses*
> *a kerchief draped over his head*
> *and flung over his shoulder.*
> *He has a cupcake with a lit candle in it.*
> *Using a big black dildo as a microphone*
> *in the style of Marilyn Monroe*
> *he begins to sing "Happy Birthday."*
> *ESTA opens her eyes.*
> *She can barely contain her joy.*

WILLY:
Happy birthday to you.
Happy birthday to me.
Happy birthday to us.

WILLY & ESTA:
Happy birthday to uuuuuuus.

> *He sticks the head of the dildo*
> *in his mouth.*
> *They both collapse in laughter.*
> *This subsides.*

WILLY:

> I love my birthday!
> It's like the world sayin –
> do me!

ESTA:

> I know.
> I love it.
> And I don't mind getting older.
> I never miss the year before.

WILLY:

> If I was a girl
> I'd be just like you.
> If you were a boy
> you'd be just like me.

ESTA:

> I know.

> *WILLY is gone.*

> *ESTA alone.*
> *A sad smile.*
> *She removes her birthday hat*
> *and blows out the candle.*

> *A dog barks a warning.*
> *ESTA is gone.*

> *RICOTTA alone*
> *on her veranda*
> *cradling a quart of scotch.*

RICOTTA:

> Cleo! Quiet!
> Stop it Cleo!
> Now!

The barking stops.

Who's there?
Who the hell is there?!

The dog barks.

Cleo!

The barking stops.

CAMILLA:
It's Camilla.
It's Camilla Milley from across the road.

CAMILLA appears.
She is holding a baking pan.

RICOTTA:
What?
Are you here to gloat?

CAMILLA:
I brought you a pan of Rice Krispies squares.

RICOTTA:
Laced with rat poison?

CAMILLA:
I thought about it.

RICOTTA:
If you're here to collect a bit more dirt
for your rumour mill:
I'm a wreck.
I haven't bathed in days
and all I do is drink
and talk to myself.
Things can't get much worse.
I'm pretty well spent.

Sufficient?
Now why don't you go find
someone else to eat alive.

CAMILLA:
I'd like to say I'm sorry.

RICOTTA laughs.

RICOTTA:
What are you up to Camilla?

CAMILLA:
Over the years I've –
I've gotten great pleasure out of other peoples' pain.
I've taken comfort in others' failure and –

RICOTTA:
And?
Do you actually expect me to be your confessor?

CAMILLA:
I don't expect anything I –

RICOTTA:
You've been rattling my cage for years Camilla Milley.
I owe you nothing.

*After an awkward moment
CAMILLA offers the pan of squares.*

I don't eat either.

*RICOTTA pours booze over the squares.
CAMILLA withdraws the pan.*

CAMILLA:
I'll leave you alone.

RICOTTA:
Good idea.

CAMILLA is gone.
RICOTTA alone.

The dog barks.

Cleo! Quiet!

WILLY appears.

That damn dog.

WILLY:
She's just protecting you.

RICOTTA:
She's just driving me crazy.

> *RICOTTA is looking out*
> *as if into a mirror*
> *putting a bit of make-up on.*
> *WILLY looks over her shoulder*
> *as if into the mirror*
> *passing her what she needs from a small make-up bag.*

WILLY:
Why do you wear make-up anyway?

RICOTTA:
So I won't scare my co-workers.

WILLY:
You don't need it.
You're so beautiful already.

RICOTTA:
I already like you Willy.
No need to try to get on my good side –
cuz there isn't one.
But you're pretty sweet for sayin that.

Every girl should be so lucky –
to have a little fag hangin around.

WILLY:

I guess women must get tired
of gay guys callin them beautiful.
Like – what's it mean really?

RICOTTA:

Everything!
That is a huge untruth.
It's impossible for a woman to tire of being called
beautiful –
by cocksucker or not.
If dogs could speak we would blush and say thank you.
But then again –
most men are dogs who can speak:
ironic.
You're pretty beautiful yourself Mister.

WILLY:

I don't feel beautiful.
I'd like to be handsome but –
I'm just cute.

RICOTTA:

Cute is good.
If you weren't so young
and I wasn't so tired
I might even try to seduce you myself.

WILLY:

Age means nothing.

RICOTTA:

Say that and mean it twenty years from now.

WILLY:
> I'm not attracted to people my age.

RICOTTA:
> Are you flirting with me?

WILLY:
> I always flirt.
> I can't help it.
> It's just natural.

RICOTTA:
> You make me a little envious baby.
> I was a flirt and a half back in the day.
> And I don't regret any of it.
> Enjoy it while you can.
> Go for it.
> Be a bitch.
> Guys love a bitch.
> Mind you –
> their wives don't.

WILLY:
> I wish I was funny like you.
> I wish I had a sense of humour.

RICOTTA:
> You really don't need a sense of humour –
> until your looks start to go.

WILLY:
> I have a memory of one of my first moms –
> my favourite.
> I was five or six.
> I used to sit on the counter
> in the downstairs bathroom –
> I guessed we were rich
> cuz there was a bathroom up and down –

and watch her put her make-up on.
Just sat there watchin her
like we are now.
I think I was happy then.
But she wasn't happy –
even I knew that.
And him –
the dad –
he was more like a visitor.
I liked it there while it lasted.
I had my own room.
She read me stories.
She woke me up.
She hugged me.
But then she got sick and I had to go.

RICOTTA:

You're brave Willy.
You keep stepping up to the plate.
Good things are in store for you.
I believe that.

WILLY:

I'm chronically hopeful.

RICOTTA:

Yes you are.

WILLY:

Did you ever want to have kids?

RICOTTA:

Nope.
Too selfish for that.

WILLY:

Seems all the wrong people have the kids
and all the right people don't.

RICOTTA:
    I don't think that's entirely true.
    But it's still not a point I would argue.

WILLY:
    You and Bernie are perfect.

RICOTTA:
    I don't know about perfect.
    Lucky maybe.
    But nothin comes easy.
    You gotta work at it.
    Hard. All the time.
    You just don't find a soul mate –
    you have to invent them.
    Cuz love at first sight sure don't last.

WILLY:
    He's awesome Bernie.

RICOTTA:
    Yeah –
    for an asshole he's pretty awesome.
    But I ain't no Pollyanna.
    That's for fuckin sure.
    Okay –
    what should we have for supper tonight?
    You've watched me make that Caesar salad enough
    to do it on your own right?
    And we'll warm up that chicken potpie.
    Done.

WILLY:
    He's great in bed I bet.

RICOTTA:
    He's better on the floor.

        They laugh.

What are you doin
havin thoughts like that about my old man?
Listen here you little homo
careful where you bat those eyelashes of yours.

WILLY:
Everyone thinks about that.
They're liars if they say they don't.

RICOTTA:
True enough.

WILLY:
I love you guys.
You really did save my life you know.

RICOTTA:
And a life worth saving.

> *Silence.*

WILLY:
Do you wanna kiss me?

> *Silence.*

RICOTTA:
Willy –
go make the salad.

> *WILLY is gone.*
> *RICOTTA alone.*
> *She ponders the memory.* ·
> *Pause on this.*
>
> *The dog barks.*

Cleo!
Shut the fuck up!

The barking stops.

Music in:
"Up"
by Shania Twain.

RICOTTA is gone.

Crude coloury ricocheting light.
Stud Cité.
WILLY's first performance.
Beyond the beaded curtain
he is nervous.
He wears cute underwear
and dirty white socks
with a hole in the toe.

He musters his courage
and comes through the beaded curtain
almost stumbling.
He dances
an awkward
though sweet routine –
a mish-mash
from his jazz dance camp days:
gallops
chasses and pas de bourrée –
not exactly the stuff of jaded seduction.
He rubs at his crotch
trying to get hard
smiling
shrugging his shoulders.
He babbles incoherent apologies
to the audience
embarrassed
smiling bravely through it all.

He continues to dance
wiggling and writhing his way
to the front of the stage
but takes one step too many
and begins to fall from the stage.
BERNIE rushes in
catching him
wrapping him in a blanket.

The music
and ricocheting light
dissolves.

BERNIE and RICOTTA
stand over WILLY
who is passed out on their floor
wrapped in a blanket.

RICOTTA:
You bring them back here now.
You rub it in my face.

BERNIE:
He's hurt.
He needs a place to sleep.

RICOTTA:
You bring them back here –
to our home?
Have I become that numb?
Am I that stupid?
Will the real dumb cunt please stand up?
Present.

BERNIE:
Ric
it's the Porter kid from out the road.

RICOTTA:
  Oh I know who he is.

BERNIE:
  He needs a place to sleep.

RICOTTA:
  And so do you.
  Get out.

BERNIE:
  Ric.

RICOTTA:
  Take him and go.

BERNIE:
  He's hurt.

RICOTTA:
  Who isn't?

BERNIE:
  It's not what you think.
  I love you.

RICOTTA:
  And I love you.
  Out.

                WILLY comes to.

WILLY:
  Mom?
  Is that you Mom?

RICOTTA:
  For Christ's sake –
  what is it with you fuck-ups
  and your mothers?

I'm not your mother kid.
I'm nobody's mother.

WILLY passes out.

You've crossed the line Bernie.
This is too much even for a well-adjusted fag hag.

BERNIE:
You're not a fag hag.

RICOTTA:
Oh –
so you're not a fag?

Silence.

BERNIE:
He needs help Ric.
He's been beaten up.
I found him passed out by the shed.
The cops are at that poor kid's house
twice a month.
You know what goes on there.
We'll get in touch with someone
who can help him in the morning.

Silence.

It's not what you think.

Silence.

RICOTTA:
Put him in the spare room.

*BERNIE and WILLY
are gone.*

RICOTTA alone
lost in the memory.
She gazes into the sky.
The dog barks.

You're lookin for a trip to dog heaven Cleo!
Shut! Up!

Music in:
ambient slutty hip-hop.

WILLY and FLOAT
leaning on the bar
wearing professional underwear
and trendy runners.
It's a slow day at Stud Cité.

WILLY rubs his chest
continuously
unconsciously.
FLOAT drumming his fingers on the bar
chews on a straw.

Lost in thought
they stare off.
Tedium rules.

WILLY:
   Remember making those masks
   out of brown paper bags?
   Cutting out the eyes with small square scissors
   or just poking your fingers through?
   Colouring it
   and gluing sparkles and yarn on it.
   I never drew on a mouth.
   I licked my way through
   after I put it on my head –

chewed the bits of paper up
and swallowed it.
Then your tongue popped out
and someone always laughed.
It was an invisible feeling
forgetting what you looked like
but still knowing who you were.
Except braver.
I felt braver.
Or happier.
I don't know.

FLOAT:

Rogue –
you're getting weirder every minute.

WILLY:

I know.
I think I'm trapped in the past.

FLOAT:

People are talking.
Even the clients are wondering what's up.
Someone says hi
and you ask them if they still wet the bed.

WILLY:

I know.
I'm speakin without thinkin.
I'm sorry.

FLOAT:

Don't ask the clients
if they still wet the bed.
Because the only action you'll get
will be wet.
You hear me?

WILLY:
　　Yeah.

FLOAT:
　　And I don't think that's what you're after.

WILLY:
　　No.

　　Silence.

　　Anyway –
　　I made one of them masks last night.
　　Put it on.
　　Sat in my kitchen.
　　Seemed like hours.
　　First time I was calm in a long time.

FLOAT:
　　See?
　　That's weird.
　　That's fucked up.

WILLY:
　　I know.

FLOAT:
　　And it's kids stuff.
　　That's kid's stuff.
　　That's being a kid.
　　You're not a kid.
　　We're not kids anymore.

WILLY:
　　But it's a defining moment.
　　Don't you remember any defining moments as a kid?

FLOAT:
　　I remember getting my first blowjob
　　and realizing life was worth living.

Other than that
I can't remember that far back.

WILLY:

It's all I can think about lately –
how I got from there to here.
How I got from a bunk bed
in Batman pajamas
to here.
What happened in between?

FLOAT:

Maybe you were dropped on your head.
I don't know.

WILLY:

You really don't remember anything?

FLOAT:

Crisse Rogue –
are you writing a book?
Calice – moi patience!

WILLY:

Sorry.

Silence.

I've been thinkin more and more
about tryin to find my real mother.
I always planned to find her
and tell her where I was
when I got to wherever I was goin.
I thought I might find her
and send for her –
send her a plane ticket to meet me somewhere.
Somewhere sunny.
But I didn't.

FLOAT:
> Hold on –
> where do you go?

WILLY:
> When?

FLOAT:
> When you fuck off for a few days.
> When you come back
> you say you were visiting your mom.

WILLY:
> No.
> I just go to bed for a few days.
> Or sit up.
> Sometimes I just sit up –
> all night into the next day.
> I just zone out.
> I think about her
> but no
> I don't visit her.
> I don't know her.
> I don't know where she is.
> Sorry.
> Don't tell anyone okay?

FLOAT:
> I got better things to do
> than talk about your skinny ass.

WILLY:
> I didn't mean to lie.

FLOAT:
> Whatever.
> We're all liars here.

WILLY:
Thanks Float.

Silence.

FLOAT:
You just sit up all night?

WILLY:
Yeah.

FLOAT:
Wearing that fucking mask?

WILLY:
I only did that once.
I just started doin that.

FLOAT:
Maybe you should stop.

WILLY:
I guess it was like meditation or somethin.
I don't know.
It kinda kept me together.

FLOAT:
Hate to tell you –
it didn't.

WILLY:
No.
No long term effects unfortunately.
Just when I have it on.

FLOAT:
Too bad.

Silence.

WILLY:

I'm havin a little trouble separatin – things.
And I know that.
And I'm bringin it to work with me.
And I know that.
I should be separatin things.
Real life. Work life.
I know. I mean –
I know I've been weird.
It's not like I don't know.
I know.
Maybe I gotta quit here.
Maybe I gotta quit this.
I don't know how much longer I can do this.

FLOAT:

You make good money.
You're popular – when you're focused.
They ask for you.
Pisses us off sometimes.
But we like you.
Me and the other guys like you Rogue.
You're a likable guy.
That's a big plus in this fucking snake pit.

WILLY:

I try to be nice.
I try to be myself.

FLOAT:

I know.
You're just saying some weird shit lately.

WILLY:

I know.

FLOAT:

So stop it.

Silence.

WILLY:

You know that regular of mine?
Just likes to talk?
Buys everyone drinks?
Maybe has one dance?

FLOAT:

Fat guy shaved head
les yeux cross side?

WILLY:

No. No that's Maurice.
"You got an ass as smooth as a J-cloth" Maurice.
It's like working at a petting zoo with him.
This guy's good lookin.
Could probably get whoever he wants.
But maybe he can't.
He's shy.

FLOAT:

He just likes to pay for it.
C'est tout.
Less complicated.

WILLY:

I guess.
Anyway I enjoy our time.
He treats me like a person.
At least he's not always tryin
to get his finger up my ass.

FLOAT:

That's a plus.

WILLY:

Anyway
I said hi to him on the street.

I saw him on the street and said hi.
He ignored me.

FLOAT:

What? He hurt your feelings?
You're letting them hurt your fucking feelings?

WILLY:

No.
But I said hi.
I just said hi.
I was just tryin to be a regular fuckin person
who says hi to people.
And he ignored me.
And yeah okay –
it did kinda hurt.
I'm not made of stone.

FLOAT:

He's probably married Rogue.
She was probably right there –
coming out of a store.

WILLY:

He said he wasn't.

FLOAT:

And you believed him?
Que c'est ça hostie
what are you thinking?

WILLY:

I don't know.
I really don't know.
My feet aren't on the ground.
I don't feel safe.

FLOAT:

Safe?

What's safe?
There's nothing safe.
We're never safe.
If you ever thought you were
you were in denial.
And if you ever were –
it was false.

WILLY:

I don't even know you.
You don't know me.

FLOAT:

Are you eating?

WILLY:

Yeah I eat.
But I'm tryin not to eat junk.
I like Caesar salad.
I make it myself sometimes.
And I eat soup
cuz my stomach is nervous.
Did you ever just boil an onion with garlic?
It's amazing how good it is.

FLOAT:

That's not eating.

WILLY:

I'm kinda on a fast.
I'm in search of a spell
for clearer vision.

FLOAT:

Now that's fucked.
That's weird.
You have to eat.

WILLY:

    I do.

    Everything's just weighin heavy on me though.

    I'm losin track of the stories I tell.

    I'm not keeping them all straight in my head –

    ya know?

    I'm forgettin –

    names and stuff.

    More than usual.

    People like to be remembered.

FLOAT:

    Some of them don't fucking deserve to be remembered.

    Like that fucking psycho –

    tried to stiff me for a hundred bucks?

WILLY:

    Don't know.

FLOAT:

    Last week.

    A fucking historic moment.

    He seemed sane at first.

    Well

    he was talking to himself –

    that should have been a clue. Anyway –

    I'm just trying to get my money

    and he keeps saying

    you're not Willy

    and I keep saying

    no I'm not Willy

    you wanted to call me Willy

    but I'm not Willy.

    And he keeps saying

    where's Willy

    and I keep saying

    there's no fucking Willy here.

And on it goes –
where's Willy I need Willy.

WILLY:
What did he look like?

FLOAT:
Drunk.
I don't know.
I just wanted my money.
And I'm just about to ask him again
and he says
do you believe in heaven?
and I say
heaven?
been there done that got the halo –
I got hell on my mind.
Trying to make a joke.
Then he says he's worried about me
that he's sorry
and that he loves me
and that he always loved me.
And he wants to save me
rescue me
take me away and save me from myself.
Fuck –
condescending
patronizing
hypocrite bullshit fuck.
I mean you deal with it all the time and let it slide but –
I just wanted my fucking money.
Then he gets all –
sur la défensive –
and says
don't give me that pretty boy cock tease bullshit.
And I say

cock tease? this is a fucking strip joint –
get with the fucking program!
Give me my fucking money hostie!

And he leaves.
He gets up and leaves.
Stumbles away.
I have to get dressed and run after him.
I don't have any cash.
Slow night.
I don't even have money to take a taxi home.
I see him running into that –
la petite ruelle –
just off the park there.
Pis là je cours mon gars –
I'm running hard.
He could run. The fucker.
Couldn't walk but he could run
en sacrament –
wailing and screaming.
Fucking crazy.

I catch up.
He's staring up at the sky.
He's got his shirt and pants off
fucking dancing around
babbling –
waiting for the fucking Mother Ship I guess.
Crazy
schizo-fucking-frénique man.
Then he looks at me with this stunned fucking look –
doesn't recognize me with my clothes on –
and he drops to the ground.
Dead.
I guess.

WILLY:
>   Dead?

FLOAT:
>   I don't know.

WILLY:
>   What did you do?

FLOAT:
>   Went through his pockets
>   called the cops
>   and ran.

WILLY:
>   Maybe he was still alive.

FLOAT:
>   Maybe he still is.
>   I don't know.
>   That's why I called the cops.
>   I didn't have to call the cops.

WILLY:
>   What did he look like?

FLOAT:
>   I don't know. Fucked up Anglo
>   closet case drunk –
>   who doesn't pay.
>   What? don't look at me like that.

WILLY:
>   Like what?

FLOAT:
>   Hurt.
>   You're too sensitive man.
>   You need to toughen up.
>   You're getting too sensitive.

I'm being realistic.
I'm not trying to fuck anyone over.
I don't want to hurt anyone.
But people will walk all over you
if you let them.
I'm just trying to take care of business.
Take care of my self.
Because there is one thing I know for sure –
the deck of cards of life
dealt me a tough hand.
It hasn't been easy for me either Rogue:
hidden aces
jokers that look like kings.
But that's okay.
You play what you got.
I'm not complaining.
And I don't give up.
And I get what's mine.
And I use what I got –
which is a big uncut cock
and a nice smile baby.
You like my smile baby?

FLOAT smiles and winks at WILLY.

WILLY:
You have beautiful lips.

FLOAT:
Exactly.
They're all so sad and romantic.

WILLY:
You do.
You have beautiful lips.

Willy moves in to kiss Float.

Float stops him
with a palm to Willy's chest.

FLOAT:
> Hey man –
> come back to earth.

WILLY:
> What?

FLOAT:
> What? You tried to kiss me.
> You just tried to kiss me –
> is that a joke?

WILLY:
> I don't know.
> Is it funny?
> If it's funny I guess it's a joke.
> Is it funny?

> *Silence.*

> I think I'm gonna cry.

FLOAT:
> Sacrament.

WILLY:
> No.
> No I'm okay.

FLOAT:
> You got to get off the crack.

WILLY:
I'm not on crack.
I'm not on nothin.
Which makes it all the stranger.

FLOAT:
Whatever you say.

WILLY:
I'm sorry.

FLOAT sees a potential customer.

FLOAT:
Hey!

WILLY is gone.

Hey there handsome –
you're being good I hope.

He squeezes his crotch.

Ooooo –
my underwears is too small all of the sudden.

He flirts
winking and licking his lips
then gesturing
for the customer to follow him.
FLOAT is gone.

WILLY
beyond the beaded curtain
bare chested in blue jeans
sits in his chair
hands crossed at the wrists
in his lap.

WILLY:
This is not delirium.

*WILLY approaches the beaded curtain.
He never steps through
but plays with the strands
at times peeking through –
straddling both worlds.*

In these troubled times I am grateful –
for my mirror ball.

I leave my place to start my day.
I don't have a home.
I have a place.
I leave my place to start my day.
The day is long and uneventful.
I look at books through windows.
I ponder the history of a pigeon.
I think about love
and what that means for someone like me.
I wonder if I'll get out of the trap.

Then –
I spy an old mirror ball in a dumpster.
This makes me smile.
I take the mirror ball and head back to the place.

I pause at the door as usual.
I know I'll feel like a stranger when I go in.
I always do.

I go into the place.
I cover the windows with old beer cartons.
I hang the mirror ball from the ceiling.
I splice some wires
and plug it in.
It works. It spins.

I duct-tape my flashlight to the door frame
aiming it at the ball
turn out the overhead light and –

    A mirror ball spins.

and it's excellent.
It's like it was always meant to be.

I put on my mask
and sit in my favourite chair –
my only chair.
I feel complete comfort.

The first few days without food are the hardest.
But starvation feeds the imagination.
When I get cold
I discover
that if I cross my arms
at the wrists
in my lap
heat shoots through my balls
and up my spine.
The pain in my belly subsides.
The freckled light from the mirror ball
is like warm rain.

Hunger is my friend.
Freedom is near.
The cracks between the worlds widen.
It's all so amusing.
Giggles purr in my tiny stomach.
It's all so funny and sweet.

I think and think.
Every thought is important:
war is inevitable –

asparagus is from the lily family.
All thoughts are equal.

And I think about the spider
and how she protected me.
And how sometimes the sky is the ocean.
And I think about you.
I think about all of you.

This is not delirium.

> *WILLY is gone.*

> *BERNIE alone.*
> *He sips a bottle of beer.*
> *After a moment*
> *RICOTTA enters*
> *dressed for work*
> *comfortably conservative*
> *in not so comfortable shoes*
> *carrying groceries.*

RICOTTA:
Hey honey.

BERNIE:
Hey babe.
Good day?

> *They kiss.*

RICOTTA:
Long.

> *WILLY appears*
> *in his standard jeans and t-shirt.*
> *He carries his sheatshirt over his arm.*

BERNIE:
    Hey Willy.

WILLY:
    Hello Mr. Gillis.

BERNIE:
    If I've told you once –

WILLY:
    Bernie.

RICOTTA:
    Willy's gotta piss like a racehorse right?
    He's gonna stay for dinner.
    One of us will run him in later.
    Go ahead Willy.
    Don't worry about your shoes.

WILLY:
    Thanks.

        He leaves his sweatshirt
        on a chair
        and exits.
        RICOTTA *waits till she is sure he is gone.*

RICOTTA:
    I'm worried about him Bernie.

BERNIE:
    Why?

RICOTTA:
    He just seems so distant.
    Not a peep out of him at work –
    in days.
    He's usually so bright –
    chatting everyone up.
    We were actually getting compliments

about deliveries being on time.
But all of a sudden he's distant.
He can barely look me in the eye.
Just go for a walk with him –
down by the river.

BERNIE:
Sure.

RICOTTA:
And ask him about his new apartment.
I think he's pretty proud of it.

> *RICOTTA exits.*

BERNIE:
What are we havin?

RICOTTA:
Grabbed some wing steaks at IGA.
Just gonna throw them on the barbie.
My fuckin feet are killin me.

> *After a few moments*
> *WILLY appears.*

BERNIE:
So how ya doin?
New job.
New apartment.

WILLY:
It's more like a room.

BERNIE:
New room.

WILLY:
It's great.
It's small.

But it's mine.
Thank you again for all your help.

BERNIE:

No problem Willy.
But we do miss having you around here.

Silence.

So you're good?

WILLY:

Yeah.

BERNIE:

You don't sound convinced.

WILLY:

Sorry.

BERNIE:

Don't be sorry.
You want a drink or anything?

WILLY:

No I'm good.

BERNIE:

So what's goin on?

WILLY:

Not much.
I'm always a little weird this time of year.
I noticed that the last few years.
I guess it's normal.
Seasons changing.
My allergies are still hangin on.
So I'm a little off balance.
It's normal. It's just –
I'm thinkin too much.

Got a lot on my mind.

BERNIE:
  Like what?

WILLY:
  Nothin. I mean –
  I just kinda feel like I'm –
  like I'm livin two different lives or somethin.
  What I think and what I do are –
  are different.
  Or somethin.
  Like I'm not plugged in.
  Like I'm not plugged into –
  what I'm thinkin and what I'm doin.
  Like what I'm thinkin and what I'm doin –
  are different.
  I don't think I'm thinkin what I'm doin
  or doin what I'm thinkin.

BERNIE:
  If we all did what we thought
  we'd all be in jail.

      BERNIE laughs.
      Silence.

  I'm sorry Willy.
  I didn't mean to make a joke.
  I didn't mean to laugh at what you're feeling.

WILLY:
  No problem.
  It is kinda funny.
  I self-analyze too much.

BERNIE:
  You're a deep thinker.
  That's a good thing.

Silence.

Decide what you want to do after the job finishes up?

WILLY:
I think travel.
Maybe end up in Montreal.

BERNIE:
Sexy city.

WILLY:
Yeah.
That's what I hear.
I'd like to learn French maybe.

BERNIE:
I'm sure you'll absorb it like a sponge.

WILLY:
Hope so.
But I don't know what I want to do.

BERNIE:
Haven't found your passion yet.

WILLY:
No way.

BERNIE:
Well –
that doesn't happen overnight.

WILLY:
No.
I like hearin stories
about people who discover what they love
when they're like forty. Ya know?
When it comes more naturally over time.

BERNIE:
　　People change hats
　　hundreds of times in a lifetime.

WILLY:
　　I never felt my age anyway.
　　Never related to people my age.

　　　Silence.

　　But you love what you do – right?

BERNIE:
　　Well if you asked me twenty years ago
　　where I saw myself today
　　I sure wouldn't have said
　　livin in the country
　　makin cheese and raising chickens.

WILLY:
　　But you love it?

BERNIE:
　　I love being my own boss.
　　I love working outside.

WILLY:
　　Yeah.

BERNIE:
　　Yeah.

　　　Silence.

BERNIE:
　　When you say you um –
　　feel like you're living two different lives what –
　　what do you think you mean when you say that?

WILLY:
I think I just need to go away.

BERNIE:
Change is good.

Silence.

WILLY:
I love you.

Silence.

BERNIE:
Um –
we love you.

Silence.

WILLY:
I love you.

Silence.

BERNIE:
What?

WILLY:
I'm in love with you Mr. Gillis –
Bernie.
I'm in love with you
and I can't pretend
and I don't know what else to do
or what else to say
except
I love you.

Silence.

BERNIE:
> Um.
> I'm married.
> I'm a married man.

WILLY:
> I love you.

>> *Silence.*

BERNIE:
> I'm married.
> I'm a married man.

WILLY:
> I love you.

>> *Silence.*
>> *All still.*
>> *Then WILLY runs off*
>> *leaving his sweatshirt behind.*

>> *Silence.*
>> *All still.*

>> *BERNIE grabs WILLY's sweatshirt*
>> *almost runs after him*
>> *but doesn't.*
>> *He buries his face*
>> *in the sweatshirt*
>> *inhaling deeply*
>> *then holds it to his chest.*

>> *RICOTTA appears*
>> *barefoot.*

RICOTTA:
> Where's Willy?

BERNIE:
> He said he had to go.
> He forgot he had to go.

RICOTTA:
> He can't walk that far.

BERNIE:
> He said he wanted to.

RICOTTA:
> What did you say to him?

BERNIE:
> Nothing.
> He had to go.
> He said he had to go.
> He forgot his sweatshirt.

RICOTTA:
> It's mild out.

> > *She takes the sweatshirt from* BERNIE.

> What did he say?
> What did he say to you?

BERNIE:
> He said he had to go.
> And he went.

RICOTTA:
> Something is goin on.
> I don't know.
> Well –
> I hope you're hungry.

> > *RICOTTA is gone.*
> > *BERNIE alone.*

Music in:
"Can't Run from Yourself"
by Tanya Tucker.
BERNIE begins to move with the music.
Constrained at first
building to an aggressive strip tease.
He rips off his shirt.
He grabs his jeans at the waist
they are tear-away
and come off at one fell swoop
so he is left gyrating
in his briefs.
He howls at the sky
then suddenly
he falls to the ground
and lays there
motionless.

ESTA comes through the beaded curtain
followed by FLOAT.
She carries a bowl of lemons.
Her hair is wet.

FLOAT
in sweats
leans at the bar
counting twenties
with the expertise of a bank teller –
at least four hundred bucks.

ESTA sits at a table.
She squeezes fresh lemon juice into her hair
and distributes it.
Juice runs down her cheek.

FLOAT's cell phone rings.
He rolls up the bills
takes his cell phone from his sock
replacing it with the cash.

ESTA rubs the juice into her face.
The actions become ritualistic.
She squeezes juice on her shoulders.

FLOAT checks the incoming call
rolls his eyes
takes a breath
and answers.

FLOAT:

Pour some sugar on me!

I'm sorry.

Don't be angry.

I'll be right there.
I'll make it up to you.

He hangs up.
He looks scared.

ESTA reveals a breast
squeezing lemon juice over it
and massaging.

CAMILLA
comes through the beaded curtain.
She stops in her tracks.
She punches herself in the stomach
and smacks herself in the face.
She repeats these actions.
Then still.

RICOTTA
comes through the beaded curtain
she arrives on her veranda
with her ever-present glass of scotch.
Music out.
The plaintive cry of a loon.
RICOTTA puts the glass to her lips.
She reconsiders.
She pours the booze on the ground.
She smells something pleasant in the air.

RICOTTA:
Everything
undiscovered
before me.

Music in:
"Here You Come Again"
by Dolly Parton.
The mirror ball spins.
Beyond the beaded curtain
WILLY is isolated in a warm light.
He sits in his favourite chair
arms crossed at the wrists
in his lap.
He is naked.
He is wearing a paper bag mask
with kooky childish eyes made of buttons
and fits of yarn for hair.
There is no visible mouth.
The chair moves
glides
through the beaded curtain.
Beaded strands play over WILLY's shoulders.
WILLY's tongue
pops through the paper mask.

WILLY stands.
He moves with the music.
His fingers
as if playing over the beaded strands.

BERNIE
manages to get himself
to hands and knees.
He sees WILLY
and begins to crawl toward him.

The lights
fade to black.